Copyright
© 2019 by Rachel Hill. All rights reserved.

No part of this publication may be reproduced, stored, or transmitted in any form or by any means, electronic, mechanical, photocopying, recording, scanning, or otherwise, except as permitted under Section 107 or 108 of the 1976 United States Copyright Act, without the prior written permission of the author.

Requests to the author and publisher for permission should be addressed to the following email: **Rachel@RachelTravels.com.**

Limit of liability/disclaimer of warranty: While the publisher and author have used their best efforts in preparing this guide and workbook, they make no representations or warranties with respect to the accuracy or completeness of the contents of this document and specifically disclaim any implied warranties of merchantability or fitness for particular purpose. No warranty may be created or extended by sales representatives, promoters, or written sales materials.

The advice and strategies contained herein may not be suitable for your situation. You should consult with a professional where appropriate.

Neither the publisher nor author shall be liable for any loss of profit or any other commercial damages, including but not limited to special, incidental, consequential, or other damages.

This Travel Planner & Journal Belongs To:

_____

How To Use Your Travel Planner

The Few Next Pages are Written Examples of How to Utilize This Travel Planner.

~~Bucket~~ Life List!

ACTIVITY   DESTINATION

- [ ] Dogsledding & Snowboarding — Arctic Circle, Finland
- [ ] Sky Diving — Dubai, UAE
- [ ]
- [ ]
- [ ]
- [ ]

Travel Essentials Pre-Filled Travel Packing List

Destination(s)	# of Days	Weather
South Africa	8	Spring (67-75*)

- ☐ ID/ Passport
- ☐ Visa (if needed)
- ☐ Copies of Documents
- ☐ Money & Credit Cards
- ☐ Electronics
- ☐ Chargers/ Converters
- ☐ Boarding Passes
- ☐ Insurance
- ☐ Shower Shoes
- ☐ Sungalsses
- ☐ Jacket
- ☐ Underwear
- ☐ Socks
- ☐ Bras
- ☐ Scarf/ Sarong
- ☐ Makeup Kit
- ☐ Sanitary Items
- ☐ Hair Essentails
- ☐ Scarf/ Sarong
- ☐ Washcloths
- ☐ Umbrella
- ☐ Toilet Paper/ Wipes
- ☐ Medicine Kit
- ☐ Glasses/ Contacts
- ☐ Walking Shoes
- ☐ Lighter/ Matches
- ☐ Laundry Bag
- ☐ Jewelry

Destination Planner

Destination   **RT Flight Cost**

- [ ] Johannesburg, SA $1,178/pp
- [ ] Cape Town, SA $1,278/pp
- [ ]

Sightseeing

- [ ] SAFARI: 2 days/ 1 night
- [ ] Hike Table Mountain (Cape Town)
- [ ] Walking Tour- Soweto (Jo'Burg)
- [ ]
- [ ]
- [ ]

Fun Facts About Destination

1) South Africa's drinking water is rated 3rd best in the world for being "safe and ready to drink".

RT = "Round Trip"

Restaurants to Try

Breakfast/Brunch

#Coffee Is Life Cafe - In the city center

_____

_____

_____

Lunch/Dinner

Cave Restaurant - Dinner in a cave/ need reservations

_____

_____

_____

Bars/ Happy Hour

The Rose Bar - speakeasy style bar near hotel

_____

_____

_____

Accommodations

Accommodation Option 1:

The Hilton Grand - $245/nt (City Center)

Serves free breakfast

In the city center (can be noisey)

Has a gym and sauna!

Accommodation Option 2:

Accommodation Option 3:

Daily Travel Itinerary

Today's Date

My Goal(s) For Today Is.
- [ ] Meet a local !
- [ ] See all the sights on the list for today
- [ ]

Schedule

Morning:

Have breakfast at #Coffee Is Life Cafe

Visit The Museum of Anthropology

Afternoon:

Evening:

Notes:

Guides & Checklists

The Following Are Blank Pages of Guides & Checklists

Travel Packing List

Destination(s)

Weather

# of Days

Travel Packing List

Destination(s)

Weather

# of Days

Travel Packing List

Destination(s)

Weather

# of Days

~~Bucket~~ Life List!

ACTIVITY   DESTINATION

- [ ]
- [ ]
- [ ]
- [ ]
- [ ]

~~Bucket~~ Life List!

ACTIVITY   **DESTINATION**

- [ ]
- [ ]
- [ ]
- [ ]
- [ ]

~~Bucket~~ Life List!

ACTIVITY **DESTINATION**

- [ ]
- [ ]
- [ ]
- [ ]
- [ ]

Your Travel Planning

Destination Planner

Destination   **RT Flight Cost**

- [ ] _____
- [ ] _____
- [ ] _____

Sightseeing

- [ ] _____
- [ ] _____
- [ ] _____
- [ ] _____
- [ ] _____
- [ ] _____

Fun Facts About Destination

- [ ] _____
- [ ] _____
- [ ] _____

RT = "Round Trip"

Restaurants to Try

Breakfast/Brunch

_____

_____

_____

_____

Lunch/Dinner

_____

_____

_____

_____

Bars/ Happy Hour

_____

_____

_____

_____

Accommodations

Accommodation Option 1:

_____

_____

_____

_____

Accommodation Option 2:

_____

_____

_____

_____

Accommodation Option 3:

_____

_____

_____

_____

Daily Travel Itinerary

_____
Today's Date

My Goal(s) For Today Is. . .
- [ ]
- [ ]
- [ ]

Schedule

Morning:
_____
_____

Afternoon:
_____
_____

Evening:
_____
_____

Notes:
_____
_____
_____

Today's Reflections

Daily Travel Itinerary

_____
Today's Date

My Goal(s) For Today Is. . .
- ☐
- ☐
- ☐

Schedule

Morning:
_____
_____

Afternoon:
_____
_____

Evening:
_____
_____

Notes:
_____
_____
_____

Today's Reflections

Daily Travel Itinerary

Today's Date

My Goal(s) For Today Is. . .
- [ ]
- [ ]
- [ ]

Schedule

Morning:
_____
_____

Afternoon:
_____
_____

Evening:
_____
_____

Notes:
_____
_____
_____

Today's Reflections

Daily Travel Itinerary

_____
Today's Date

My Goal(s) For Today Is. . .
☐
☐
☐

Schedule

Morning:
_____
_____

Afternoon:
_____
_____

Evening:
_____
_____

Notes:
_____
_____
_____

Today's Reflections

Daily Travel Itinerary

Today's Date

My Goal(s) For Today Is. . .
- [ ]
- [ ]
- [ ]

Schedule

Morning:

Afternoon:

Evening:

Notes:

Today's Reflections

Daily Travel Itinerary

_____
Today's Date

My Goal(s) For Today Is. . .
☐
☐
☐

Schedule

Morning:
_____
_____

Afternoon:
_____
_____

Evening:
_____
_____

Notes:
_____
_____
_____

Today's Reflections

Destination Planner

Destination   **RT Flight Cost**

- [ ] _____
- [ ] _____
- [ ] _____

Sightseeing

- [ ] _____
- [ ] _____
- [ ] _____
- [ ] _____
- [ ] _____
- [ ] _____

Fun Facts About Destination

- [ ] _____
- [ ] _____
- [ ] _____

RT = "Round Trip"

Restaurants to Try

Breakfast/Brunch

_____

_____

_____

_____

Lunch/Dinner

_____

_____

_____

_____

Bars/ Happy Hour

_____

_____

_____

_____

Accommodations

Accommodation Option 1:

_____
_____
_____
_____

Accommodation Option 2:

_____
_____
_____
_____

Accommodation Option 3:

_____
_____
_____
_____

Daily Travel Itinerary

_____
Today's Date

My Goal(s) For Today Is. . .
☐
☐
☐

Schedule

Morning:
_____
_____

Afternoon:
_____
_____

Evening:
_____
_____

Notes:
_____
_____
_____

Today's Reflections

Daily Travel Itinerary

_____
Today's Date

My Goal(s) For Today Is. . .
- [ ]
- [ ]
- [ ]

Schedule

Morning:
_____
_____

Afternoon:
_____
_____

Evening:
_____
_____

Notes:
_____
_____
_____

Today's Reflections

Daily Travel Itinerary

Today's Date

My Goal(s) For Today Is. . .
- ☐
- ☐
- ☐

Schedule

Morning:

_____

_____

Afternoon:

_____

_____

Evening:

_____

_____

Notes:

_____

_____

_____

Today's Reflections

Daily Travel Itinerary

Today's Date

My Goal(s) For Today Is. . .
- [ ]
- [ ]
- [ ]

Schedule

Morning:
_____
_____

Afternoon:
_____
_____

Evening:
_____
_____

Notes:
_____
_____
_____

Today's Reflections

Daily Travel Itinerary

Today's Date

My Goal(s) For Today Is. . .
☐
☐
☐

Schedule

Morning:

_____
_____

Afternoon:

_____
_____

Evening:

_____
_____

Notes:

_____
_____
_____

Today's Reflections

Destination Planner

Destination   **RT Flight Cost**

- ☐ _____
- ☐ _____
- ☐ _____

Sightseeing

- ☐ _____
- ☐ _____
- ☐ _____
- ☐ _____
- ☐ _____
- ☐ _____

Fun Facts About Destination

- ☐ _____
- ☐ _____
- ☐ _____

RT = "Round Trip"

Restaurants to Try

Breakfast/Brunch

_____

_____

_____

_____

Lunch/Dinner

_____

_____

_____

_____

Bars/ Happy Hour

_____

_____

_____

_____

Accommodations

Accommodation Option 1:

_____
_____
_____
_____

Accommodation Option 2:

_____
_____
_____
_____

Accommodation Option 3:

_____
_____
_____
_____

Daily Travel Itinerary

_____
Today's Date

My Goal(s) For Today Is. . .
- [ ]
- [ ]
- [ ]

Schedule

Morning:

_____

_____

Afternoon:

_____

_____

Evening:

_____

_____

Notes:

_____

_____

_____

Today's Reflections

Daily Travel Itinerary

Today's Date

My Goal(s) For Today Is. . .
- [ ]
- [ ]
- [ ]

Schedule

Morning:
_____
_____

Afternoon:
_____
_____

Evening:
_____
_____

Notes:
_____
_____
_____

Today's Reflections

Daily Travel Itinerary

_____
Today's Date

My Goal(s) For Today Is. . .
☐
☐
☐

Schedule

Morning:
_____
_____

Afternoon:
_____
_____

Evening:
_____
_____

Notes:
_____
_____
_____

Today's Reflections

Daily Travel Itinerary

Today's Date

My Goal(s) For Today Is. . .
- ☐
- ☐
- ☐

Schedule

Morning:

_____

_____

Afternoon:

_____

_____

Evening:

_____

_____

Notes:

_____

_____

_____

Today's Reflections

Daily Travel Itinerary

_____
Today's Date

My Goal(s) For Today Is. . .
- [ ]
- [ ]
- [ ]

Schedule

Morning:

_____

_____

Afternoon:

_____

_____

Evening:

_____

_____

Notes:

_____

_____

_____

Today's Reflections

Destination Planner

Destination   **RT Flight Cost**

- [ ] _____
- [ ] _____
- [ ] _____

Sightseeing

- [ ] _____
- [ ] _____
- [ ] _____
- [ ] _____
- [ ] _____
- [ ] _____

Fun Facts About Destination

- [ ] _____
- [ ] _____
- [ ] _____

RT = "Round Trip"

Restaurants to Try

Breakfast/Brunch

_____

_____

_____

_____

Lunch/Dinner

_____

_____

_____

_____

Bars/ Happy Hour

_____

_____

_____

_____

Accommodations

Accommodation Option 1:
_____
_____
_____
_____

Accommodation Option 2:
_____
_____
_____
_____

Accommodation Option 3:
_____
_____
_____
_____

Daily Travel Itinerary

_____
Today's Date

My Goal(s) For Today Is. . .
☐
☐
☐

Schedule

Morning:
_____
_____

Afternoon:
_____
_____

Evening:
_____
_____

Notes:
_____
_____
_____

Today's Reflections

Daily Travel Itinerary

Today's Date

My Goal(s) For Today Is. . .
- [ ]
- [ ]
- [ ]

Schedule

Morning:

_____

_____

Afternoon:

_____

_____

Evening:

_____

_____

Notes:

_____

_____

_____

Today's Reflections

Daily Travel Itinerary

_____
Today's Date

My Goal(s) For Today Is. . .
☐
☐
☐

Schedule

Morning:
_____
_____

Afternoon:
_____
_____

Evening:
_____
_____

Notes:
_____
_____
_____

Today's Reflections

Daily Travel Itinerary

Today's Date

My Goal(s) For Today Is. . .
☐
☐
☐

Schedule

Morning:

_____

_____

Afternoon:

_____

_____

Evening:

_____

_____

Notes:

_____

_____

_____

Today's Reflections

Daily Travel Itinerary

_____
Today's Date

My Goal(s) For Today Is. . .
☐
☐
☐

Schedule

Morning:

_____

_____

Afternoon:

_____

_____

Evening:

_____

_____

Notes:

_____

_____

_____

Today's Reflections

Destination Planner

Destination　　　　　　　**RT Flight Cost**

- [ ] _____
- [ ] _____
- [ ] _____

Sightseeing

- [ ] _____
- [ ] _____
- [ ] _____
- [ ] _____
- [ ] _____
- [ ] _____

Fun Facts About Destination

- [ ] _____
- [ ] _____
- [ ] _____

RT = "Round Trip"

Restaurants to Try

Breakfast/Brunch

_____

_____

_____

_____

Lunch/Dinner

_____

_____

_____

_____

Bars/ Happy Hour

_____

_____

_____

_____

Accommodations

Accommodation Option 1:

_____

_____

_____

_____

Accommodation Option 2:

_____

_____

_____

_____

Accommodation Option 3:

_____

_____

_____

_____

Daily Travel Itinerary

_____
Today's Date

My Goal(s) For Today Is. . .
- ☐
- ☐
- ☐

Schedule

Morning:

_____

_____

Afternoon:

_____

_____

Evening:

_____

_____

Notes:

_____

_____

Today's Reflections

Daily Travel Itinerary

_____
Today's Date

My Goal(s) For Today Is. . .
- [ ]
- [ ]
- [ ]

Schedule

Morning:

_____

_____

Afternoon:

_____

_____

Evening:

_____

_____

Notes:

_____

_____

_____

Today's Reflections

Daily Travel Itinerary

_____
Today's Date

My Goal(s) For Today Is. . .
☐
☐
☐

Schedule

Morning:
_____
_____

Afternoon:
_____
_____

Evening:
_____
_____

Notes:
_____
_____
_____

Today's Reflections

Daily Travel Itinerary

Today's Date

My Goal(s) For Today Is. . .
- [ ]
- [ ]
- [ ]

Schedule

Morning:
_____
_____

Afternoon:
_____
_____

Evening:
_____
_____

Notes:
_____
_____
_____

Today's Reflections

Daily Travel Itinerary

Today's Date

My Goal(s) For Today Is. . .
- ☐
- ☐
- ☐

Schedule

Morning:

_____

_____

Afternoon:

_____

_____

Evening:

_____

_____

Notes:

_____

_____

_____

Today's Reflections

NOTES

Made in the USA
San Bernardino, CA
25 February 2020